Humanosecuritus:
Information Security is ~~90%~~ all about people

DEDICATION

This book is dedicated to our dear wives, Renata and Ivana.
To our parents and kids.

CONTENTS

ACKNOWLEDGMENTS

We would like to express our gratitude to all those who provided support, talked things over, read, wrote, offered comments, allowed us to quote their remarks and assisted in the editing, proofreading and design.

1

INTRODUCTION

The world is currently experiencing an unprecedented technological revolution. We are witnessing a great increase of new and different ways in which technology is influencing and impacting human life. Mobile apps, social networking, the digital economy, Web 2.0, etc., are just a few keywords that redefine the way we do things at all levels in life. What about information security? In this fast-paced race to determine who will do more in less time, it seems that we are forgetting some basic elements that should be present to secure the whole chain, making a system safe and secure. The time taken to develop a new mobile app has been reduced to a strict minimum.

Customers do not want to wait for a programmer to write an entire code from scratch and they expect the final product to be ready in the minimum amount of time. Today, programmers do not really complain about these demands and do what the majority of programmers on the planet are doing: they use freely available libraries and frameworks to speed up their programming. These insecure programming practices should cause worry and be a concern for each of us who are using the open source software in our daily lives. A report from Aspect Security[1] shows that 80% of today's applications comes from libraries and frameworks. This means that only 20% are a product of an author's original work. This circumstance is a clear indication that the human factor controls the security chain and if people fail to secure it, the entire chain will fail; such an outcome, in turn, can compromise the entire organizational information system.

Another paradigm that is changing our lives relates to the shift from physical to digital objects. Or it might be better to describe it as the shift from the physical world to the digital world. The way we search for information, the way we engage in social interactions with people, and all other physical means of information exchange have radically changed in recent years. These changes have happened so quickly that one might wonder where the end is. At what price are these changes occurring? Have our privacy protections improved? Can we still trust all the big brands, such as Google or Microsoft, while knowing the kind of privacy, compliance, and trust challenges that have arisen with all of these speedy

[1] https://www.aspectsecurity.com/news/the-unfortunate-reality-of-insecure-libraries/

changes? The consumerism of IT has allowed everyone to bring smartphones into the organizational environment, but it should be noted that consumers still want the same kind of user experience where simplicity, ease of access, and a straightforward authentication process are the norm.

The topic of security complexity has grown in its importance and has been given more attention than ever. Securing the 10% is no longer that difficult because an organization usually does have the knowledge, tools, and platforms to put in place the toughest security measures possible. But how can an organization effectively secure the remaining 90% remaining where humans play the critical role? This is where the complexity comes into play because before securing humans, we may need to understand why they do not comply with protocols. Are security awareness trainings effective? Do employees pay attention to them?

It is clear that the weakest link is humans. The human factor plays a crucial role and is the first line of defense against cyberattacks. On one side, it is rather easy to protect information against the human factor as long as it stays in the company, but how can information be protected when faced with an employee who was just fired and took with him potentially dangerous records and information? A recent example from a Fortune 500 company has shown that when an employee leaves a company, it takes about three months to cut all authorizations. This means that this particular ex-employee was still able to log into the organization's internal system, a situation caused by complex internal HR systems where several approvals at different levels are needed to remove an employee from various internal systems. In smaller companies, this process is much faster since the entire process usually relies on only one or two IT persons who can react very quickly to such developments. One might wonder how such big companies could have complex internal HR systems where an "ex-employee" processes is not eased along the entire approval chain. As it stands with many companies, if only one human forgets to submit an approval on just one day, thereby not complying with the approval process, then the company faces a real security risk.

Should CEOs be worried? Generally speaking, CEOs do not really care about the company's security; that is the reality. One IT security guy once told me that I was not complying with the company's IT policy since he had detected that I had installed Skype—which was strictly against company policy. So I called him to further understand why I could not use this nice, handy application and while we talked, he finally said that he would close his eyes to this and would unofficially allow me to keep Skype. He said, "If the CEO can have it, why not you?"

I asked him, "Does that mean the CEO also has Skype?" He explained that not only did the CEO have Skype, but he also had dozens of other unapproved applications. When he told the CEO that he was going to remove all of the unapproved applications, the CEO said that he because he was the CEO, he needed the applications. If we think about a top-down approach to security, where approaches to security should come from top, then this example feels a bit scary since the real question is, if the CEO does not care and is not worried about security, should I be?

Are security awareness trainings working? Many times you have been asked to complete an online security training but how many times did you really read the content? Didn't you just do "click, click, next, next..."? Why is that so? Why is it that employees do not read through security training materials? One could argue that there are too many of them and that generally, they are not visually appealing or interesting. Another possible argument could be that employees do not have the time to spend on such activities. Then again maybe the answer is linked to the previous topic about CEOs. What would happen if employees could see that their CEO also (attentively) completed all of the assigned security trainings? Would the employee care more? Nevertheless, security trainings and the education of employees remains one of the strongest tools used to cope with the 90% human factor related security challenges.

The latest security threats involving the human factor have not change very much in their nature. They have changed in their complexity and execution by shifting from the physical to the digital world; information has simply become abundant. Facebook, Twitter, and LinkedIn are just few a jungles of information that make it much easier to collect valuable details that could be exploited by malicious attackers. How are organizations responding to these employee breaches? Do they have any mechanisms in place to better monitor, track, and analyze the external threats related to their employees' activities?

Digital business is a reality where connectivity is omnipresent. It would be difficult to imagine one day without being connected. There is also a clear transition occurring from the physical human to the digital human as the digital side of humans invade their professional and private lives. The impact of this invasion is that the border between the physical and digital is now often unclear.

Bring Your Own Insecurity (BYOI) can be defined as the infiltration of human insecurity into the business environment. Basically, people do not feel threatened until they become victims. Only when you have had a bad experience you will start paying attention and taking more care to prevent possible risks. Until then, it is clear that insecurity will reign.

Dual-use technology reflects the two opposite sides of technology use: its negative and positive sides. GPS is a good example of this duality. Initially, GPS was used for military purposes, while today, it is mostly used for civilian reasons. When it comes to the latest technology trends, such as private smartphone use to retrieve company emails (the BYOD, Bring Your Own Device, trend), there are also two sides: positive—the employee may be more productive and more flexibility can be achieved, and negative—malicious software can be installed on the employee's own device, which may cause important security risks if the device is connected to an organization's information system.

Humanosecuritus - or Human security - questions whether information security is all about people. How can we protect humans from themselves? If we reference and build upon the famous Pareto principle with reference to information security, it turns out that 90% of the threat comes from people and only 10% is about the underlying security technology.

Example: The smaller 10% could represent the technology that enables employees to access their corporate intranet through their mobile devices. The entire authentication and encryption process would be provided by the technology. The remaining 90% could correspond to employee behaviors such as the way they secure their mobile devices by making sure they do not lose the device, complying with the existing procedures and processes, and not installing any unauthorized apps, etc.

Should you care about security? You are a simple employee and the security laws are not in your job description—should you behave in a carefree manner or should you approach this the way you would when thinking about the security of your loved ones or someone you care about? Security can and should be looked at from an emotional standpoint because that could be the magic formula in how to decrease risk.

The following chapters will explore all of the above topics, providing useful directions and guidelines that will further help us better understand why human security is the key to successful information security. Or, more precisely, why today's security trainings and education materials are not effective and what should be changed to make the topic of security more relevant to an employee. In other words, we will figure out why employees should care.

┌─────────────┐
│   2   │
└─────────────┘

THE SHIFT FROM PHYSICAL TO DIGITAL

The shift from the physical world to the digital world has already occurred. In just few years, at an incredible place, we saw objects shifting from one side to the other without us properly understanding the change at its most basic levels.

Work habits shift

The way we work, where we work, and how we work have been dramatically reshaped. From physical locations we have moved to become quite ubiquitous; the workplace is now where the connection is. If I can connect, I can also work. And not only it is about connectivity but above all, it is about smart connectivity because the new wave of smart devices has brought with it smarter ways to connect.

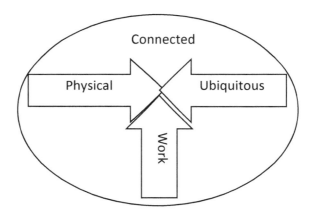

Figure 1. Work habits shift

On the Figure 1 we can see the clash between the physical world, the ubiquitous world, and the workplace. The commonality between all of them is that they have been connected.

People want to be connected—this is surely a part of their nature so the right question is when to disconnect and say it is enough. Is it even possible to do that in today's connected world? This work habits shift brings an entirely new dimension to the way we secure our job environments. Not so long ago, it was enough to secure and protect only internal organizational assets where the principle was: what's inside was internal and was by definition protected. Today, this huge border has disappeared and a new definition might be: what is coming from outside is very dangerous and we are not really ready to safeguard ourselves against it. In this paradigm shift, organizations are usually scared and avoid opening their gates to the outside world. However, the challenge is the fact that this outside world is coming from the inside—from the organization's employees. This situation opens a Pandora's box that calls for completely new ways of dealing with security.

Fortunately, so far, it seems that companies have been rather welcoming of this paradigm shift and most of them are encouraging their employees to change along with it. Given that this is still a rather new phenomenon, we will probably witness different trials, successes, and failures. In 2013, Yahoo announced that they had asked all their employees who were working from home to return to their physical offices. This move could results in some interesting outcomes if it turns out that this work habits shift could be better controlled.

Personal security vs. organizational security

Organizational security used to be a closed loop, where once you got in, you were just putting another brick in a wall that was already strongly secured and would not fall. At least it wouldn't have in a simple way. The idea was that employee security was less important than organizational security, which had to be created on strong foundations. Today, personal security is king. If you want to connect using your smartphone to check your email, you need to be protected and authenticated, and your communication needs have to be secured. If you want to download a new mobile productivity application, someone needs to verify, check, and approve that your application is safe enough and will not endanger anything on the organizational side. The same logic goes for any other employee end point attempt to access organizational information systems—protection needs to occur from end to end. However, how can an organization check every single new mobile application when there are not only thousands of new productivity applications every day, but also dozens of different versions of the same already approved application?

Organizational security has become a complex environment that includes both internal and external personal security factors (Figure 2).

Enterprise firewalls are usually the gold standard to keep the enemy at the gates. Huge investments have been made into hardware and software firewall solutions with the idea in mind that a firewall should stop most potential attacks. But in the "personal security" context, the enemy is no longer at the gates, the enemy can easily pass through them with the simple employee's help.

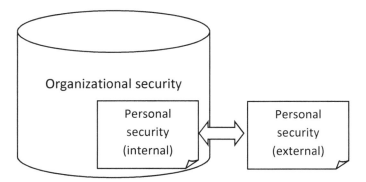

Figure 2. From personal security to organizational security

Are firewalls still needed? The simple answer would be yes. The more complicated answer would be: yes, but it is not enough anymore by itself. Maybe a new type of firewall is needed where every time an employee introduces his mobile phone into the organizational ecosystem a smart type of firewall scanning can be conducted. Something much like when you cross a baggage check zone in the airport where the machine is scanning you could become a necessity. In any case, what is known is that a revolution is needed.

Are we ready for it? The very first step is that employees need to understand the underlying challenges and become more aware of the risks they bring with them every time they click the connect button on their devices.

"Social" and "Cloud": two words we should be aware of

One thing is sure: both social media and cloud-based services are the new realities and as such will not simply go away. It is also not a question of whether they will be adopted or not, and at what scale, but rather how fast the evolution will be. In these two new virtual spaces, people tend to forget the basics of freedom and democracy and most of them completely neglect their rights. Privacy, trust, and compliance are among the most cited concerns, risks, and challenges when it comes to social- and cloud-based activities. Still, awareness and ignorance are omnipresent. We either do not care or do not want to care, or perhaps we simply believe that bad things will not happen to us on an individual level. The best experiences are those that have been lived—and this is what can explain the ineffectiveness of security trainings. Many organizations do have security awareness trainings on various topics, from compliance down to security basics, but if you ask employees what really they loved about the trainings, they will tell you, "When I clicked next, next, next, till arriving to the end..." It is definitely not about the content or visual attractiveness of these trainings, but rather about the fact that people do not care about the subject because they do not believe it concerns them. Until a personal security breach does happen. So what can we do? How can we make the learning process more effective?

Soldiers are taught to be soldiers through trainings involving shooting real guns and being placed in very realistic war situations. And these approaches work. Doing the same with employees can be a very effective method in leveraging security awareness and knowledge. And employees will surely appreciate it. This reminds me of Michael Douglas in the movie, *The Game*, where he missed the challenges in his daily life and was dragged into simulated dangerous life situations. The moral of the story is that his understanding, perception, and appreciation of life changed.

It is the right time to change your training strategy and do trainings in more simulated environments. We can no longer rely on the typical "Click next" trainings where employees do not really care and do not see any added value to their attentive participation. Changes in the approach to security is a must and has to start now.

Today social media and cloud-based services pose very real threats, and tomorrow there will be something else that we will need to understand and adapt to in a faster, better, and smoother way. If we want to keep or build a competitive advantage, adapting our organization and security context to the changing times are the keys to success. Without such action we are prone to failure.

Economic and social aspects

Hacking was funny. Hacking was nice. Hacking was a game. Hacking was knowledge. Today, hacking is much more than that. It has become many people's main jobs. A job means money and when money speaks, it means that hacking has taken on new dimensions and brings with it more dangerous stakes where well-organized and funded organizations are becoming major threats. We have seen apparitions of new hacker organizations that claim to be driven by certain causes. Anonymous hacking organizations are just one kind among them. The issue with these trends is that they can have very dangerous and devastating effects on an organization. Moreover, people oftentimes sympathize with them and indirectly support them.

Figure 3. Shift in hacking motives

We have definitely seen a shift from the simple physical hacker who used to sit in his dark room, trying to hack into someone's PC during long nights, to the digital hacker who is now generally paid, has ambitious goals, and has important resources at his disposal. This digital hacker can be extremely dangerous, not because there are financial reasons behind his act or because in many cases he is a part of a group of well-organized digital hackers, but rather because the attacks are very advanced and persistent. This is the latest trend called APT, Advanced Persistent Threat.

Another red alarm for employees to stay vigilant and careful about when it comes to their own digital security is the economic and social aspects that appear to be the top drivers in this new security paradigm. Interests are changing and adapting to our new economic realities, where the nature and size of security breaches are rapidly changing and turning into something unseen so far. These are the real threats knocking on our doors. Will we be able to deal with them? Only the future will show us the answer. Still, we should not wait for that future to come and knock on the wrong door, which could very well be yours. In the meantime, you should get ready and be prepared since security risks are getting tougher, are more dangerous, and are coming from literally everywhere.

3

SECURITY COMPLEXITY

Not so long ago in order to authenticate yourself in an organizational system, a simple username and password combination was enough. All you had to do was choose a fairly complex password and it was believed that you were safe and that all of the organization's information was protected.

Today, this is no longer enough. Due to the explosion of services and number of users on different online platforms, users have been placed in a situation where they have to have dozens of different usernames and passwords to accommodate every service or tool. And as is always the case, humans would not be humans if they were not just a bit lazy; many people have started to pick very simple passwords. In Table 1 you can see the top used passwords. The list was compiled from various files of collected stolen passwords that were posted online by hackers. These files contained millions of passwords.

#	Password	Change from 2011
1	password	Unchanged
2	123456	Unchanged
3	12345678	Unchanged
4	abc123	Up 1
5	qwerty	Down 1
6	monkey	Unchanged
7	letmein	Up 1
8	dragon	Up 2
9	111111	Up 3
10	baseball	Up 1
11	iloveyou	Up 2
12	trustno1	Down 3
13	1234567	Down 6
14	sunshine	Up 1
15	master	Down 1
16	123123	Up 4
17	welcome	New
18	shadow	Up 1
19	ashley	Down 3
20	football	Up 5
21	jesus	New
22	michael	Up 2
23	ninja	New
24	mustang	New
25	password1	New

Table 1. SplashData's "Worst Passwords of 2012"

It is evident that the old situation had to change and more security in the authentication process was needed.

This additional security brought a new complexity to the field where the authentication market over the last few years has simply exploded with a number of new solutions and products aimed at leveraging the existing authentication processes. While this trend is very welcome since security is being improved, on the other side, we have put all of the complexity on the human factor by creating two-, three-, or multi-factor authentication processes. Such tasks now ask humans to remember not only a username and password but also to do something else (e.g. iris or fingerprint scanning) that will enable their authentication. So is security getting simpler? We believe that technology is getting more robust, simpler, and more secure but the complexity of the process is being put on human shoulders because now people have to satisfy two or more authentication requirements. While there is no doubt that the achieved level of security can be very high, it is also incontestable that there is still an important path ahead to better understand the underlying complexity as it relates to data privacy, ethical dilemmas, identity proofing, etc. In other words, what will happen to our personas if someone steals our digital fingerprint? How will we be able to protect our privacy in this highly complex environment?

Once again, humans are at the core of this new, complex security evolution. One would maybe expect to have a more technology-driven solution where human intervention would be factored in at a minimum. Instead, an individual currently needs to remember some portion of a password (or an entire one), to put his fingerprint on a device, to look after his mobile phone and make sure it is not stolen, and so on. One day we will probably witness an era where humans will just say a voice command and with a set of complex verifications, they will be authenticated. "Viva Las Vegas!"—I can't wait for that day since my gut feeling is that we are creating beautiful technology but are also making an even more beautiful complexity.

Managing security complexity

The rising complexity of software and hardware parts in the security ecosystem is making it harder for IT departments to effectively manage their security assets, which is clearly bringing greater risk to the vulnerabilities that are not being properly addressed. The Web and social media applications are just another brick that adds to the complexity of the situation. Despite the fact that many organizations have introduced appropriate policies and blocked the usage of social media applications, risks have not disappeared. On the contrary, employees invest time in trying to bypass these restrictions and look for different ways to gain control to restricted content. It is time to simplify and consolidate security management with the final objective of having simple, efficient, and clear security policies in place that employees can easily follow.

But is it really all about the policies? Even policies were as simplified as possible, would people truly follow or read them? If you are working in a large international company, it could be interesting to conduct a small survey and go around asking different people in various positions about the organization's existing security policy and where it can be found. I ran such a survey. No one had any idea about the existing security policy or where to look for it. Again, we argue that it is not about the policy but rather about the organizational culture; the culture is what dictates how to behave in specific situations. It is like when children come home from school and the first thing you teach them to do is to wash their hands. There is no policy for that. It is also not written anywhere. It is just a culturally inherited thing where you constantly told your kids that washing their hands is matter of health and that it will kill all bacteria.

Forget about the hundreds of pages of policy—rather, organizations should focus on scaring their employees by telling them what can and will happen if they do not do things the proper way. Gaining security by threatening is the way to go because it is the only efficient way to properly manage security complexity.

Security by threatening

In other words, this could be called "emotional information security," which represents the varying degrees of an employee's emotional state in relation to the information security risk. In order to decrease and better control security complexity, a new and different approach is needed. In this approach, a very light brainwash of employees is needed to make them understand that not only their own security is in danger but also the organization's. Employees usually do not care much about their own security because they do not fully understand the risks associated with breaches, but they should care about the organization's security. Oftentimes employees are apathetic to both. Threatening employees, while respecting their rights and privacy, is the best method to achieve a heightened awareness and less reliance on technology. How can you do it? There are a number of ways. One way would be to have live simulations of hacking attacks and demonstrate what can happen when an individual's privacy and security is breached. Insisting upon and having repeated exercises are important factors in this approach. Revisiting our example of children washing their hands, if you tell them only once to wash them, they will do it, but if you do not insist that they maintain this habit, the children will give up and think that the effort is useless and unnecessary.

Complexity as the worst enemy of security

Many will agree that complexity is definitely the worst enemy of security. But how did we come to face this complexity? Did we create it or was it naturally caused? If we put aside the complexity and take a step back to reflect on how this complex situation was created, we could probably better understand the causes that have led to our current situation. Yes, complexity is the worst enemy of security but it did not come from thin air. It did not appear from nowhere.

It was, once again, created by us—humans. We complicated the simple things through our inventing and reinventing, designing and redesigning. As soccer players would say, "Stop the ball and think twice." Another view of the situation could be the also that sees complexity as an opportunity as generally complexity may lead to new innovations. So maybe, just maybe, we could use this complex situation and see how the security component could benefit from it. This development could be a new innovation that will enable a kind of super system that would provide superior security and risk protection.

For now, we will have to be more vigilant and see how to get to the next level where simplicity is ruling. We will also seek to better understand the role of the human factor, which is the beginning and end of the entire chain. The right question is: is the weakest link the human factor? And if so, what can be done to make it less weak and stronger?

4

THE HUMAN FACTOR—THE WEAKEST LINK

The German Enigma machine from WWII was considered an unbreakable system during its time. With over a quadrillion possible encryption combinations for every message, it would take millions of years to crack a simple message. Yet due to the human factor, the Enigma was compromised. A lack of good training led to procedural mistakes where operators were entering very simple "daily keys" such as "AAA." It took some time before the Germans understood that the human factor was what had caused the compromise, not the Enigma itself.

In today's world, not a lot has changed. Technology has progressed remarkably and provides very high levels of security, but how secure can you be if an employee inadvertently reveals his login and password details to external people? You cannot put a piece of software protection on the human factor and make it secure. We tend to forget this and leave the situation as is without worrying too much about the consequences. While there is no secret formula for how to manage the human factor, it is very clear that more action needs to be taken.

We argue that it will be difficult to play with human nature and push humans to be more careful and sensitive about what they do. Instead, since the human factor is the weakest link, maybe the best method would be to remove humans entirely from the chain. By this I do not literally mean completely removing them but rather limiting and fully restricting what they can do. If they are part of the link, then they should become a special link inside of a big chain. There is one issue with this approach—in practice, it is very difficult to do. When you think about the top employee's riskiest practices, you come down to actions like accessing the Internet via unsecured wireless networks, not removing confidential information from computers, sharing passwords with others, using the same username/password with different websites, using generic USB keys, leaving computers unattended when outside the workplace, etc. So removing or limiting any of these practices may turn out to be very difficult. Many of them might even end up being impossible tasks to accomplish because this is the way that today's modern jobs are organized.

The special human link

Instead, creating a special human link is a necessity. Employees needs to be held accountable and responsible for any single action they do. By creating awareness around accountability and responsibility, security will gain new levels. But not just any kind of accountability or responsibility will do. It is not enough to say, "You are accountable and responsible for the actions you do or do not do." It is time to think about the human factor as just another component of the whole security ecosystem. When an employee does something illegal (i.e. surfing to a forbidden website or plugging-in a generic USB that is not encrypted), the employee may get a generic message saying, "Website access is restricted." We argue this is not the way to go and is simply inefficient because the employee will try again and again to access the blocked content. Instead, a real alarm should be raised, informing the employee about his accountability and responsibility in the actions he is about to take.

When there is hardware failure, an alarm is raised and a bunch of people are tasked to work on it, trying to fix the problem, replace a part, etc. So it is a real alarm that was raised and is solved with real people working on it. Concerning our human factor, a similar special procedure should be put in place where a real alarm would be raised with real people informing and reminding employees about the process. This plan, to be viable in organizations, would need new resources and processes. But this is the way to go.

Today, we have a jungle of highly sophisticated hardware and software, and humans who believe that it's no big deal if they do something wrong. The system may inform them of their actions and tell them that they can or cannot do this or that but that's it. What would you do? I would certainly plug in that USB or would try to see if I can still access the forbidden social media website another way.

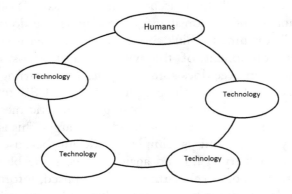

Figure 4. The human link in a security ecosystem

The special human link as part of the entire chain could bring significant savings and improvements to an organization's overall security. It just has to be thought through and implemented very carefully.

Coming back to the Enigma machine, what the Germans did was they improved the human factor by tightening their procedural flaws and focusing more on operator training. This strategy helped strengthen the Enigma's security but it did not stop the codes from being breached as the hardware part of the Enigma was became more intensely attacked.

In the same vein, better, smarter, and greater attention needs to be focused on the human factor. We could have the most brilliant hardware in place but without a good understanding of the entire security chain, we may compromise it.

In 2010, Microsoft blamed two of its employees for problems that arose when their computers were compromised and then misused by hackers to advertise for over 1,000 online pharmaceutical websites. In 2011, the state of Texas announced that records for 3.5 million persons had been left unprotected on the Internet for over a year. Finally, Gartner believes that 99% of firewall breaches are cause by incorrect configurations of the devices rather than firewall flaws.

5

SHOULD CEOS BE WORRIED?

Should CEOs be worried about the information security risks?

This is probably a controversial question since the right answer will depend who you ask. For one side, the answer is very clear: CEOs represent the biggest security risk to an organization because they underestimate the size and importance of potential threats. Moreover, there is a clear imbalance between what statistics are saying and what hard numbers say. Speaking purely based on statistics it seems that according to a recent PwC report, 42% of business leaders believe they are frontrunners in security. Surprising! Especially considering that the number of security breaches and flaws has never been higher or had greater impact. Still, according to the same report, it seems that business leaders will spend less money on security investments.

This finding is indeed a surprise and contradicts the statements from the CEOs themselves that they are the frontrunners in the security race. However, if you ask 100 drivers about how skillful they are, it is very possible that 99 of them will say they are exceptionally skilled drivers. This is the same case with security. Believing that you are the frontrunner is not enough and your complacency could be used against you.

Another study from the Lloyd's Risk Index 2013, showed that security risk is now at third place (up from 12th place in 2012) for company executives. It seems that CEOs have woken up. The report says, "Given the well-documented frequency of cyber breaches, the relatively low weighting given to cyber risk in both the 2009 and the 2011 Risk Indices suggested too many businesses were underestimating its impact. One development may be that the perception of what motivates cyberattacks is evolving: from financial crime to political and ideological attacks. 2012 saw the takedown of the Interpol, CIA and Boeing websites, the suspension of alternative currency Bitcoin's trading floor, the mass theft of passwords from professional networking site LinkedIn, the outage of the websites of six major US banks and many more."

So are we as clever as we think we are in answering these questions? I guess not since statistics, reports, numbers, and reality are often part of different worlds and should be taken with utmost precaution. One thing is sure: cyberattacks have never been more dangerous and done more harm to organizational assets as they do today.

Moreover, the CEO is the key to the entire top-down approach of having a highly secured organization. If company executives do not understand where their budgets are going and what they are being spent on then we have a serious issue. There is also the matter of why a simple employee should care about security if the bigwig sitting on top of the organization does not care about it as well. It is all about care. If I care about something, the employee will also care. Thus, no matter how big or small an organization is, the culture of being secure should be present at all levels. A good example of this is when a person takes care of his wallet and knows what consequences could arise if his wallet is stolen. In an organizational context, this wallet should correspond to a security asset; if it is stolen, the employee should know what the consequences will be for the organization and for the employee himself.

At what level should the C-level executive worry?

This is where the situation gets more complicated. In the ideal situation, every C-level executive should worry about the same thing. In reality and paradoxically, each C-level executive worries about very different things. A CEO's main concern relates to brand reputation and at what level a brand may be impacted in the case of a security breach. How will the brand survive difficult times in cases where major incidents occur? Financial executives see security risk in terms of the financial loss a company may incur. Will the price of the company's stock be impacted and to what extent? How will shareholders and investor react to the breach? Will customers still want to buy our products? These are some of the questions that financial executives are asking themselves and the way they see security risk. On the other side, the real people responsible for security within organizations (the Chief Information Officers, CIOs, or the Chief Information Security Officers, CISOs) do not really care about financial risks or brand reputation. Their main task is to ensure that all information is secured, which means preventing security incidents entirely or making sure they have a very low business impact. In this context, we have different C-level executives worrying about different kinds of the risk. Maybe that is not such a bad since it is obvious that every level has a very precise set of tasks to accomplish and worry about.

However, on the other side, it is necessary to have perfect alignment among these different executives; being on the same page would help them build a very strong business and security measures that can be fed into their enterprise risk processes and procedures. Without that unity, the risks will only be higher because the top-down approach in securing all layers may be jeopardized.

A boardroom issue

IT Security is a boardroom issue. While it may be difficult for a CEO to understand the technological terms used by security executives, we argue that understanding how technology works or what technology is, is not the way to go. Instead, a CEO should look to understand what has been done to keep information secure and what actions are still missing. What measures are in place to enable employee mobility and what kind of risks might they bring? Most importantly, are the right security policies in place and what still needs to be done to make them fully understood and applied in the workplace? IT security is definitely a boardroom issue and the place where its appropriate implementation should begin and end. Here we quote John Pescatore from Gartner who concludes, "If I could have a CEO boot camp, I'd say, 'Make sure you put security top of mind to all of your direct reports: your CFO, your CIO, your HR people, your sales people and so on.' For most businesses today the product is information and security is key. So you have to make sure that your top reports understand security is part of their evaluation. It's not just the CIO's responsibility. It is part of life for every one of your direct reports."

6

ARE SECURITY AWARENESS TRAININGS WORKING?

The usefulness of security awareness trainings is an ongoing debate. For opponents, security awareness trainings are useless and a waste of money. Their anti-training hypothesis is gaining popularity among security experts. This rather radical thinking has many respected experts supporting those moving in this direction. Bruce Schneier, a security guru, provides an example of health security where it is difficult to link behaviors to benefits. In this context, according to Bruce, health awareness training is not effective. Furthermore, Bruce wrote in his blog, "The whole concept of security awareness training demonstrates how the computer industry has failed. We should be designing systems that won't let users choose lousy passwords and don't care what links a user clicks on."

However, revisiting our Enigma example from WWII, we saw how a lack of good training caused the machine to be cracked. So training was at the core of the security issue in the Enigma's case. An interesting experiment took place in London's financial district when researchers gave out a free CD saying it was a "Special Valentine's day promotion." You can imagine how many people took this CD, went to their jobs (in many cases financial institutions), and ran it. The researchers did not put any harmful program on the CD but instead included only a small program that informed a PC through the Internet that it was executed. So is a lack of training to blame in this case or simple ignorance?

While some people would probably argue that this is not about education but rather about the fact that it should not be possible to run a CD on a PC—that any way of connecting anything that includes any external hardware should be disallowed, here, we fall into another category of forbidding or not allowing something. Generally, when you forbid someone from doing something, the individual will try to find all the possible ways to bypass the restriction. Depending on the employee's technical skills employee, this circumvention will be more or less successful. Nevertheless, we open a different topic, which concerns shadow IT and includes all of the hardware or software that is used by employees without prior IT approval. It is believed that shadow IT brings innovation and productivity. In any case, the point is that the topic of education is a highly complex one and cannot be seen just from a single angle.

We believe that the truth about the effectiveness of security awareness trainings lies somewhere in between. Not having trainings at all is probably not a very smart decision. But conducting trainings as we do it today is not a very smart decision either.

The way to go

The real question is: what is an effective training? One thing is sure—risk will always be present. There is nothing that is 100% secure and safe. So what is the best approach? Before answering that question we have to take one step back and note that organizations will never give up on traditional methods of training. Whatever form they may have, they will not stop providing standard online or offline trainings to their employees for several reasons. One reason is that they will not take the risk that executives, in the case of security breach, will be justified in asking why no security trainings were provided. Another reason is that we do not have any scientific measures confirming training's efficacy or detrimental outcomes. The third reason is that often we also provide numbers to regulators (e.g. compliance trainings) to say that training has been done so the company has remained compliant. Following these arguments, we can conclude that traditional trainings still have a long life ahead of them and that they will not simply disappear, as some security experts may believe.

Instead of killing them softly, we have to understand what makes them ineffective. When a new user registers on Facebook and is asked about privacy consent, most people blindly click on "OK" without reading any of the points that may restrict their privacy and security behaviors. People are lazy and that is the reality. Laziness combined with a lack of motivation are the two main ingredients of ineffective trainings. People want to have things done quickly without spending any large amount of time on various procedural steps. Motivation is at a low in these situations. Why should I care if I'm not paid for that? That is not in my job description and I don't really care. In order to care I need to be more motivated and less lazy. If we want to have effective training sessions, they need to scare people. Here, "scare" is being used in the sense that people have to understand the possible consequences of not complying. We are not speaking about any physical consequences but rather financial consequences. This is where employees will have their focus. If you say to each employee that part of his annual job objective is to strictly follow security guidelines, we are pretty sure they will care a great deal more and be more motivated.

In this context we propose the Efficient Training Formula (ETF):

$$ETF = (C * M * O) - L$$

C: Care   M: Motivation   O: Objective   L: Laziness

If employees care more and are more motivated, and security is an objective in their job, they will simply start caring under the condition that they are less lazy. Their laziness will be directly impacted by the care, motivation, and especially the financial objective, which should be set up as a part of the employee's yearly objectives. Many companies do have compliance objectives in their employees' annual Management by objectives - MBOs, and in this context employees need to follow compliance standards. Why not extend these objectives by applying security awareness as well?

This is definitely the way to go since it is very unlikely that organizations will give up on trainings regardless of how effective or ineffective they may be. It is also very unlikely that these same organizations will be able to secure more the technology in the short term and thus disallow the use of any external hardware or software; the complexity associated with the task may kill any attempts made here. In addition, the financial aspect may be a decisive factor against any technological improvements to better control the security ecosystem. The Efficient Training Formula, where several ingredients are combined in order to scare people and get them more motivated, is the best strategy to implement.

One issue with this approach is that it is again all about the human factor and the way we deal with it. In theory this may sound simple but in practice it is not an easy task at all. One thing is sure—employees will definitely be more cautious if the security objective is linked to their financial bonus. However, even in this case, it is still true that if just one among 1,000 employees, the entire system may fail. So we come back again to our introductory point that perfect security does not exist. The truth is that risk will always be omnipresent no matter how perfectly we secure the entire chain.

This does not mean that we should not take any action. On the contrary, organizations need to create effective training cultures and spread them all over their organizations. This will create a long-term win-win situation for each side: the employee and the organization. Employees, and consequently organizations, will be better protected and safer as we move toward the open world where connectivity is embedded in everyone's DNA. This connectivity is a part of today's and will be tomorrow's source of risk explosion, where no one will be exempted from real threats and organizations that choose to stand and watch without acting will be strongly impacted. Now is the time to act and think about cleverer ways of providing trainings.

7

THE LATEST SECURITY THREATS
INVOLVING THE HUMAN FACTOR

The IT security ecosystem is a complex system of various internal and external factors that influence the entire system's security. Figure 5 shows the complexity of this system, where human security is a key element that drives software and hardware security.

With recent technological advances, the external factors have been attacked more often than ever before. These external factors represent the context in which an employee operates outside of the standard organizational environment but at the same time is still allowed to access the internal system. Mobile technology is one example of this situation, where the employee is now free to use his own mobile device to access company data. Cloud technology is another example, where companies have opened their doors and are enabling more and more of their employees' access to external websites that provide cloud services. In this context, security threats that involve the human factor have migrated from internal to external environments and de facto, expose themselves to the entire world. Were we ready for such a big change? One thing is sure—employee acceptance of these new technologies has enabled their mobility, their innovation, and better productivity, all of which were more than welcomed. But what about the security risk?

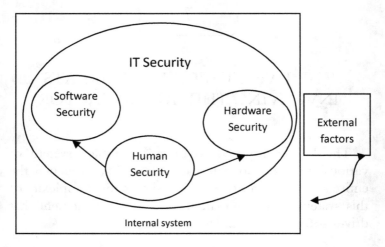

Figure 5. The IT security ecosystem

Before, hackers had to call employees and use social engineering techniques in order to gain sensitive information. Today, it is enough to use any of the social media websites, such as LinkedIn, to gain membership access to private groups and then the game can really start. Obtaining information has never been easier. Everything is connected and linked today. You have a Facebook account that will help you access another website that Facebook has provided a login plug-in for. If your initial username and password are compromised, the attacker can potentially gain access to all of your Facebook-enabled websites where you have used the Facebook login plug-in. Isn't that scary? At the end it all comes down to a trust issue. And it seems that people trust blindly without even asking the right questions in relation to this trust dilemma. "I trust Facebook," means "I trust everything else."

A study conducted at West Point Military Academy highlighted this issue with regard to authority. A fake email was sent from a fictitious colonel to 512 cadets asking them to click on the link to check their grade. The colonel's information was faked, indicating that he was located on the 7th floor of a building, which did not exist. Still, over 80% of the students clicked on the link and the majority were freshmen. Authority has a clear influence on an individual's decision-making process.

We argue that social engineering techniques are now part of a new battle field since the number of completely new sources of information and ways to get information have been made available. Social engineering has also gained in importance and definitely still represents a very real threat involving the human factor from the hacker's standpoint.

However, we believe that the human factor is the latest security threat with regard to itself. This view may sound paradoxical but it is evident that security-related matters begin and end with humans. Software is conceived by humans—likewise for their underlying mistakes. The same goes for hardware, where bugs are also introduced by humans. This is a pretty obvious way of looking at how things work.

So how can we remove the mistakes made by human themselves? A meta-human system is needed to monitor, check, and correct any human factor-related errors. This system should be able to proactively assess human behavior and act as a trustier link between the authority system, humans, and all corresponding human-produced information. Today, this kind of system is clearly missing. Can we say that Facebook or Google are our meta-human systems? Is Apple the one we should turn to? The recent NSA scandal that revealed the existence of backdoor entry points on Apple iPhones does not argue in their favor. Humanity is still on this quest for an appropriate meta-system that would be a perfect answer to our trust challenge. The Bitcoin system can be seen as a first attempt with a similar approach in the financial system, where it was conceived in a manner in which trust could be embedded. Despite the fact that some hacking possibilities do exist, we believe that we will soon see the birth of this long-awaited and much-needed meta-human system where trust, privacy, and compliance are the founding pillars and will serve as a basis for building much more secure and less risky systems.

Social engineering

Social engineering is usually used to persuade one person to reveal information that can then potentially be misused. This method has been widely discussed and analyzed in the literature. Its detailed steps have been identified as well as its countermeasures. We second the view from Mitnick and Simon, who believe that social engineering attacks are very hard to detect, which makes them almost impossible to defend against. They classified social engineering attacks into three categories: direct requests, contrived situations, and personal persuasion. With direct requests, information is directly gathered and the purpose of the request is clearly explained. The impact of this attack is not very successful because people generally do not trust these sources and will not easily reveal information when directly requested to. Contrived attacks add another layer where there attacker masks his intentions with a nice story that sounds more convincing. Personal persuasion can be classified as an attack that is hard to conduct because it requires advanced skills, calling on the attacker to manipulate an individual into believing that information is being voluntarily provided. There are other forms of social engineering attacks, such as phishing, which is usually done through emails sent with the objective of getting users to reveal confidential information (e.g. password).

Overall, the reason why these social engineering attacks are successful is because a trust relationship is usually formed with the victim. This opens the door for the security breach, where people tend to believe the attacker's claims and unintentionally provide valuable information that could jeopardize information security. We argue that the entire social media space is based on the trust link, where many people accept "Friend" invitations without doing any formal verification of people's identities. This would surely create a huge security hole since social engineering attacks have just gained an important shortcut in getting access to sensitive information. Faster, easier, and more abundant access to information has been brought about with the new open information concept in the "I trust by default" scenario where people trust by default and do not assume any wrongdoings behind other people's actions.

How can we protect ourselves?

No simple answer may be given. A lot of security experts will say that there are no effective countermeasures against social engineering attacks. Their opponents may argue with them but what about the employees who have never been victims? Why have they never been tricked? Does they have better knowledge or are there some other psychological factors that prevent them from being victims? This question calls to mind a story about a lawyer who was the victim of a phishing attack where he was asked to send money in exchange for an important prize he won in a lottery.

Despite several warnings from the point of sales employee, who was telling the lawyer that it could be a fraudulent claim, the lawyer sent three transfers in a short period before realizing that the entire thing was a scam. This story could lead to the conclusion that indeed, those saying that protection against social engineering attacks is very difficult and countermeasures are almost inexistent, may be right. However, we believe that in taking the example of the lawyer's story, the important point is that there is a very low probability that the lawyer will be tricked again. Why? Simply because he has learned a lesson; the lived experience has taught him to be more cautious next time.

The moral of the story is that it might be difficult to have countermeasures, but at the very least, by experiencing a social engineering attack, we may learn to be more careful in the event of such a thing happening to us. Thus, we believe that the most effective security awareness training is one that includes a live experience. Now the challenge is how to perform this live experience in big organizations. How can we increase awareness among 10,000 employees? That is the real challenge. We believe that the best way to do is to have a dedicated team that would be tasked with completing specific actions needed for live experience trainings. Yes, there is certainly a cost associated with creating such a team but it is one of the only ways to effectively cope with this hot topic.

8

DIGITAL BUSINESS—DIGITAL HUMANS

The race in new technological wonders will continue at an even faster pace. The Internet of Things, 3D printing, and automated judgment are just some of the newcomers that will explore and further decrease the meaning of the "analog" world. Businesses are living through a transformation and we are witnesses of the industry's reinvention. Digital business will be at core of every company strategy, which will seek to redesign and redefine the way business is done. What about digital humans? How are people impacted by this digital change? There are various terms, such as "digital native" or "digital omnivore," that speak to human digitalization.

However, the "digital human" is a much wider term and is a more connectivity-related factor where the human is in constant connected to a network. From connected TV to connected tablet. From connected mobile device to connected work environment. The only question would be: when are you not connected? Is there any minute where you are not connected?

The digital business is all about digital humans. You cannot have a digital business without transforming human behavior and thinking about going in the same direction. It might be better to say: the digital human was a prerequisite to create a digital organization because without humans there can be no organization. The risk associated with the alliance between digital business and digital humans is omnipresent and greater than before. Your digital persona, as such, is in much greater danger since everything you are in the digital world can be changed, modified, and thus illegally exploited.

We argue that we are in a digital bubble that at one moment will explode and crush in on itself, jeopardizing the entire digital business. The current situation is one where people have taken the "I don't care and I click" behavior; it is not sustainable for us and will have to be redefined sooner or later. This time of change may come sooner than we believe. It will be enough to have one major "déclic" or "trigger" to start the avalanche. I strongly believe that a combination of security factors, including compliance, trust, and privacy, will become the big trigger that will change the human mindset and make people think twice before choosing certain services, apps, or online tools. An analogy can be made with the financial crisis, which has impacted many businesses, organizations, and people. Today's technology is formidable but what price do we want to pay for continuing to use it? It's accepted so quickly with almost no real prior assessment. We blindly trust in something we do not understand. Not all big companies are facilitating this "blind acceptance" but many of them are probably unintentionally creating this bubble of digital security risk that will turn against them like a boomerang.

Today, if you do a Google search using keywords such as "travel," "tourism," etc., you will notice that the next time you go on a website that runs Google AdSense ads, you will have a similar set of thematic ads as your previous search. How did this happen? Who asked for your permission to do so? What else are you unaware of that is being done against your privacy? There are tons of similar questions that could be asked. No easy answer can be provided because the digital world, the world we are living in, has created a very complex environment where ordinary people and the majority of people simply do not care or want to know about the finer details behind such actions until one day when it is too late.

Security will guide and drive that day. Humans will become more conscious about the mistakes they were making. No organization or directive will be of a help here since these directives (e.g. the European Union directives) will never completely go against capitalistic foundations. What I find to be a paradoxical situation is the fact that many countries oblige tobacco producers to put very extreme warning messages on cigarette boxes saying something like, "Smoking will kill you," or "Smoking is bad for your health and can provoke serious illness." But if these messages are really true (we believe they are), why do we not simply forbid the sale of cigarettes? Isn't it a bit strange to say, "It will kill you if you use it," but "we will still allow you to buy it." In this context, people will continue using cigarettes because there is also the addiction factor to consider. Technology is the same with only one big difference. Addictions can be passed from one technology to another very quickly and easily. In the future, digital humans will be able to choose between so many different and great technologies that their choices will also be based on the level of security the technology brings. Recent surveys have shown that many teenagers have abandoned Facebook for other social media websites for the simple reason that their parents have also signed up with Facebook and are better able to control and monitor them. It is interesting to see how the trust relationship between users and Facebook has been lost so quickly once their parents got involved. In this matter there is a question associated with an external factor that has acted as a guardian. Surely, something similar will appear in the near future that will play a similar role of trust, compliance, and privacy.

In 2013, we saw a number of revelations concerning espionage that has been committed by American security agencies. Despite the amplitude of these occurrences, it seems that average users did not feel any real risk or threat at this time. They believed that they had nothing to hide, so the situation would remain the same. Moreover, they personally did not know anyone from these agencies and felt that no one was really interested in their online posts. Bringing parents into the equation, however, is a very different story. In this case, the impact was much greater and all of a sudden, users started to care.

The digital bubble is on its way and it is just a question of when it will hit and who will be hit. In the meantime, the digital business and digital humans are living the good old marriage. How this marriage will continue to develop, only the future will show. Bill Gates once said that we are good at predicting short-term technological advances but are very bad at predicting long-term technological evolution. Whatever happens, the digital factor will be at the center of what we do and humans and businesses will cohabit in that marriage. On the flipside of the coin there is also the "unknown" evolution of technology, which will shape this relationship and probably fine-tune it into a different form. Given that our big and beautiful nature is capable of managing its own complexity, there is no doubt that humans will try to copy the same mechanics and apply them to create a perfect synergy.

9

BYOI—BRING YOUR OWN INSECURITY

Bring Your Own "something" has been introduced in the last two years and the blank can be filled with anything from "device" to "cloud," with many different options in between. Much has been written, discussed, and analyzed regarding the security dimension of the "Bring Your Own" phenomenon. Many of the concluding points speak once again about the importance of security awareness and educational trainings. Yes, trainings and education should be included. No, they are not very efficient. In previous chapters I have explained the challenge of strictly relying on security awareness programs. Instead, we believe that the challenge is much bigger than what we have anticipated so far and what we should do is take one step back to reflect on Bringing Your Own Insecurity. In other words, the issue should be analyzed at its source. It is like a river that is polluted and we are looking at how to clean it by beginning in the middle instead of going to its source to see what is wrong.

A similar approach should be taken with employees. What has gone wrong and has been insecure from the very beginning? If we allow an employee to plug his mobile device into our organizational system, shouldn't we first maybe completely wipe out the existing operating system and install a new blank one to be sure that nothing is insecure when that same mobile device is plugged into the organizational system? If that is not something that can be done, maybe the IT department should at least thoroughly scan the employee's mobile device to look for risky behaviors. Instead, what organizations do by default is provide easy access to their systems and rely on mobile device management tools to control any risky behaviors.

Furthermore, what is undoubtedly missing is the lack of "insecurity" awareness. Taking *Inception*, the movie, as a role model, organizations should seek to plant an idea in a person's subconscious, making them aware of the possible security consequences. Why do people rarely forget their car keys? Because they know if they leave them somewhere, they will not be able to start and use their cars. More dangerously, if they forget their car keys someone could take them and steal their cars. So they do care about these items because their subconscious is telling them to care.

This difficult approach to the "inception" of an idea

could be the right strategy in achieving higher levels of security and making awareness trainings much more effective and efficient. Bring Your Own Insecurity, with its associated risks, will be better planned and analyzed. Employees will think twice before acting and this should be the final objective of this approach. Only when considering the source of the issue, while fixing it along the way, will we be able to bring additional layers of security, which is very much needed!

While this may sound like a complex task, in reality, security should be made as simple as possible. Einstein once said, "Things should be made as simple as possible, but not any simpler." In other words, the existing challenges may not be where we think they are and simplicity can probably be found somewhere else. The insecurity side of the security story is the one to look at from its creation—from the very beginning. It can be a very psychological way of looking at the problem.

Frederick the Great of Prussia said, "He who guards everything, guards nothing!" This is an elegant way to say that security today needs to be rethought, reinvented, and reshaped in its approach and the way we use mechanisms to control our external and internal assets.

We will need to rethink what an employee is and how an employee should adapt and grow with the developing technology. Transforming organizations from "Bring Your Own Insecurity" to "Bring Your Own Security" will be a long and difficult task but it is an essential path to walk. The employee should and will play the central role because at the end of the day, it is all about human security. Or most of it is about that. More careful, smarter, and better security will be guided by employee behavior. That behavior will need to be influenced, shaped, and boosted by all executives within an organization. Again, we come back to the top-down approach. Let's go back to the example of the car and the keys. Who influenced, shaped, and boosted the user's behavior so that he would take care of his keys, not lose them, not forget them, and would pay attention to them? Who planted the idea about the risks that may occur if a security breach with regard to the keys happened? Was it a kind of collective subconscious idea that was planted through various other security issues that we face in daily life? We believe that there are some standard social norms where security is one layer that is implemented by default. Why is it not the same with organizational security? Or security when going online to surf, to click on unsolicited links, or trust in unknown people over the phone? These questions are just a few in the vast number that should be answered, mostly by psychologists.

One thing is sure, the "Bring Your Own Insecurity" trend will continue in the years to come and unless we change our own attitude toward it, organizations should be afraid—very afraid. There will be no need to have a very powerful hacking tool to break into a system or to be a top-notch programmer to bypass security countermeasures because humans are their own most dangerous enemies—now and in the future. The human insecurity race is ongoing and will not end any time soon. An entire mental shift will be needed, or better yet, a huge mental shift is necessary to move things in a good direction.

Unfortunately, we are not ready for this kind of shift

and we do not want to change—until we are threatened. But that does not mean that we should wait and do nothing. IT executives should act and implement new strategic strategies that will fit with this technological evolution. More than anything else, these methods need to follow human psychological and behavioral evolution. We may need to include some factors, such as psychological ones, in the decision-making process since the world has changed along with technology and new criteria for trust, compliance, and privacy issues have since appeared. This task may turn out to be a very complex one because decision makers cannot rely anymore on simple hardware or software solutions. Instead a range of other factors need to be assessed, analyzed, and taken into account when making decisions for the future.

10

DUAL-USE TECHNOLOGY THREATS

Dual-use technology represents the technology that can be used for both peaceful and harmful aims. One example of this technology is GPS (Global Positioning System), which at the beginning was mainly used for military aims. Today, it's mostly used by civilians. However, it can be used in both directions: positive and negative. Basically, the dual-use topic concerns the dilemma of whether to use the technology or not—or better yet, the dilemma about whether to use developing technology or not.

The dual-use dilemma has been widely discussed in the

medical and military industries where the wrong choice can have disastrous effects on humans. Many people have rather positive opinions about the development of dual-use technologies despite their potential negative consequences. They argue that any development will contribute to our better understanding of the world, the way things are done, and how they can be fixed.

On the other side, opponents argue that such technologies may be used for illegal activities and can be exploited for malicious aims.

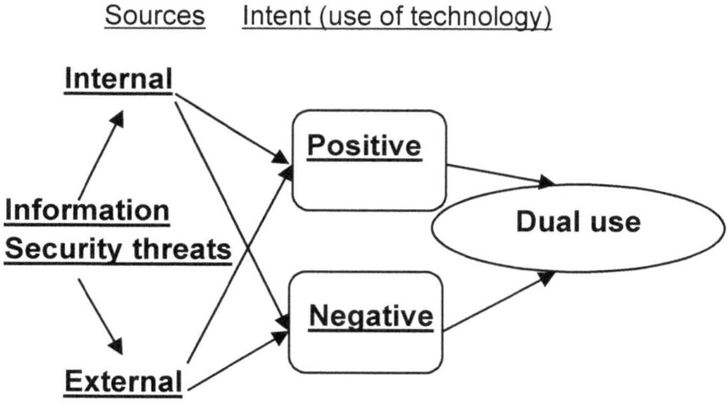

Figure 6. Dual-use technology's uses

In the computer security field, the "dual-use" dilemma has only received limited focus. Very few studies have addressed the topic. In the organizational context, dual-use technology is about the challenges, risks, and opportunities the dual-use dilemma brings. At the end of the day, it is all about security. No matter what type of dual-use technology we are introducing, security is the biggest issue concerned with its positive or negative impacts. One such example is shadow IT.

Shadow IT

Shadow IT is a currently misunderstood and relatively unexplored phenomena. It represents all hardware, software, and any other solutions used by employees inside of the organizational ecosystem that did not receive any prior formal IT department approval. With the recent mobile explosion bringing about the IT consumerism and cloud computing phenomena, shadow IT has invaded organizational systems, bringing unprecedented security risks to the IT department. Compliance issues, wasted time, inconsistent business logic, increased risks of data loss or leaks, wasted investments, etc., are just some of the potential risks that have been identified and can have important impacts on an organization's information security.

But how much do we know about this phenomena?

Given that many shadow IT applications (e.g. from smartphones, portable USB drives, or tablets) do not leave any traces behind after they have been introduced into organizational systems, it is very difficult to understand the associated risk levels. A 2012 French survey[2] of 129 IT managers classified the top shadow applications as follows: Excel Macro 19%, software 17%, cloud solutions 16%, ERP 12%, Business Intelligence (BI) systems 9%, websites 8%, hardware 6%, VoIP 5%, and shadow IT projects 3%.

[2] RESULTATS DE L'ENQUETE SUR LE PHENOMENE DU « SHADOW IT » par Thomas Chejfec: http://chejfec.com/2012/12/18/resultats-complets-de-lenquete-shadow-it/

The reality is that shadow IT is an interesting example of the dual-use challenge. It can increase employee innovation and productivity. However, on the other side, the dangers for information security are greatly increased because not knowing what, when, and how something was installed can be an IT department nightmare.

Open source software

A number of open source projects (e.g. the Nmap security scanner) are dealing with information security where their dual use raises trust and security concerns.

On the one side, black hat hackers can use it to conduct illegal activities against target networks, while on the other side, information security professionals can use it to safeguard their network by discovering security issues and potential threats. In this dual-use context, the question of trust is raised. Open source security software is a good example of the dual-use dilemma where a number of unanswered and controversial questions arise. These controversies have two sides. First, questions can be asked about who the end users are of this potentially dangerous security software. Are they hackers? Information security professionals? Second, can you trust these tools if you are using them for peaceful aims? Open source security software can be used by attackers to perform illegal activities by exploiting vulnerabilities identified on remote systems, thereby representing the negative side of their use. The positive side would be when they are used to proactively monitor and safeguard networks. This, again, comes back to a question of trust. Can information security professionals trust software developed mostly by hackers, who at the end of the day are using these same tools to add features that they need?

Trust or no trust, open source software has found its way into the enterprise ecosystem and will surely stay there for a long time.

We believe that the importance of the dual-use technologies should be leveraged among all stakeholders in the decision-making process. Regardless of whether it is a programmer who is using freely available open source libraries or a CEO who is buying new software that was created partially based on the freely available source code, everyone should be aware of the dual-use dilemma. It should be everyone's concern—not just looked at when an issue appears. It may be too late for us in this area, though.

Humans and dual-use technology

The challenge with dual-use technology so far is that no one has really even considered its positive or negative sides. When an organization is introducing new technology (e.g. mobile devices) into its information system, most of the time we only look at the positive sides. How will the technology be beneficial for employees in increasing their productivity, satisfaction, etc.? Rarely do we look at the negative sides. And even when we do look at them, we do not really try to weigh out the positive and negative aspects associated with the technology in order to better understand the risks that it may inject into the organizational system.

At the end, it is true that anything can be looked at from a positive or negative framework and many things in daily life do have dual-use components. However, in the same way that medicine is looking at the problems related to dual-use technologies, we believe that executives should also take greater interests in them.

Because we have blindly accepted and implemented a number of different technologies over recent years, we continue to lack a better understanding of the dangers and risks associated with our technology use. It is time to step up and rethink the duality of this topic in order to better understand potential benefits versus potential risks. Only by taking this critical approach can we be more confident in our decisions when it comes to the relationship between humans and technology.

11

THE 90/10 RULE

In 1906, the Italian economist Vilfredo Pareto asserted that in many events, 80% of the effects came from 20% of the causes. Basically, he created a mathematical formula that said 20% of people owned 80% of the wealth. Following Pareto's law or principle, similar behaviors have been identified in other fields.

Dr. Joseph Juran, Quality Management pioneer, found the principle of the "vital few and the trivial many," which pretty much came to the same conclusion as Pareto's work. Juran observed that 20% of something is always responsible for 80% of the results. In other words, the 80/20 rule says that 80% is trivial and 20% is vital. It also highlights the fact that we need to focus 80% of our time and energy on 20% of the work in order to be successful at managing things.

If we summarize all of the existing surveys about data and information breaches, we can conclude that the human factor is responsible for 90% of them. These surveys have identified negligent insiders, lost/stolen devices, the mobile workforce, malicious insiders, and insecure disposal as the greatest threats to sensitive data. If we take into account that security can be seen as a technological and human issue, we can say that 10% is about the technology itself and 90% is about people. While this may sound a bit trivial, as many may argue that technology is much more than that, if you think about it carefully, what is technology without people?

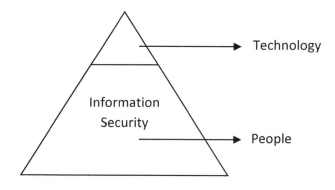

Figure 7. The 90/10 rule of information security

Going one step further, if we analyze recent data breaches, we can see that 90% of all human-related security breaches have been committed by only 10% of employees. Only a limited and small number of people are very dangerous and can potentially seriously impact organizational security.

One recent example can be found in Edouard Snowden, and despite the fact that many people have argued that what he did was not very malicious, there is no doubt that his actions were a very serious insider security breach. Another example comes from Jason Cornish, an IT administrator of Shionogi, Inc., a U.S. subsidiary of a Japanese pharmaceutical company; Cornish resigned from his position in 2010. Shortly after his resignation, the company announced that its restructuring would impact his girlfriend.

In 2011, Cornish activated software that he ran with a privileged account. The software was installed prior to his departure and resulted in the deletion of 15 virtual servers, which greatly affected the company's operations. The interesting thing about this story is that after he left the company his credentials and accounts were never removed from the company's access systems. Role-based accounts and privilege are what were missing in this scenario. In addition, it should be noted that the role-based approach is the best action that can be taken to tackle insider threats.

In nutshell, we can see that the 90/10 rule can be applied to information security, where information security is 90% about people and processes, while 10% is about the technology.

Many security professionals argue that technology should take over the balance and be much more prevalent in people's concerns. By making this shift, we would rely more on technology and less on people since secure and robust software means more security overall.

The 90/10 rule is of course just a principle and not a law, but it shows the topic's complexity give that humans mostly rely on other humans. In this scenario, everything begins and ends with humans. It is definitely time for us to rethink, redesign, and review the events that are occurring behind the curtain of the information security ecosystem.

Another point to consider relates to the interaction between the 10% and the 90%, where a strong link and relationship can be found. There is no 10% without the 90% and vice versa. It is a mutual relationship where interactivity and connectivity are very strong and cannot be separated.

You might wonder whether you should care or not. What is in it for you?

12

SHOULD YOU CARE?

The simple answer is no, you should not care about security concerns because simply put, you are an employee. You could argue that security is not part of your job description and you would expect the organization to provide the security framework. This is one angle to approach the issue from and if we take it from this side, then yes, the employee is right—carefree behavior can justified in this context. However, the problem with that logic is the fact that the organization can guarantee a lot of security points and provide a number of security measures but it cannot plant the seed of security awareness into someone's mind if that same person refuses to accept it. Another problem is that you, as an employee, need to meet some of the organization's expectations. In other words, you need to be compliant and successfully pass one or more security awareness trainings.

However, we still have an issue. It might be better to say that we have a contradiction. This carefree situation can be extremely dangerous. So should you care? We guess not yet since there is no incentive and no motivation for you to care. But if for one moment you stood still and thought this situation over—just think over—you may realize that that the organization is the place where you spend five working days per week and eight hours per day. It is like your second family. So if you think over, and compare it with your loved ones, do you care about your child security? Yes, you do. Do you care about your wife's security? Yes, you do. So why would you not care about your organization's security? The security of the same organization that is giving you a salary and helping to secure the ones you love should matter to you.

So yes, you should care about your organization's security. No training, incentive, or motivation factor will be better than the one that is already inside of you. The emotional factor is what's important.

The bottom line, in our opinion, is that it is better to look at this situation from an emotional standpoint because looking at it from any other angle may lead to a complete failure. Looking at it from the human, emotional side could be the best way to achieve the desired outcome, which is more security and less risk.

Employees need guidance even in approaching this topic from the emotional security side and how to link it to their existence. While all this talk may sound philosophical, at the end of the day, security is about humans and if we do not find the emotional link, all of our efforts may be for nothing. On the security road there are no losers or winners, only people who are connected and those individuals who do not care. There will most likely always some employees who will not care. Just as with criminals, there have been and will always be people ready to commit a crime. It is part of human nature. In this same vein, there will always be employees who are ready to protect their organizational assets and those who will not care. The big difference is that we have a chance to link everyone through an emotional chain and provide a different view of what "being compliant" and "secure" can mean. Losing a job if one is not being compliance is one example. Being accountable for not respecting security procedures is another example. It all goes back to respecting what one has at the very least partial ownership of. Small part of this company is also mine. It might be just 0.01% but still, it is mine and I need to secure and protect it—just as I do with my family.

So stay vigilant and do care!

13

FINAL THOUGHTS

Information security is a hot topic and despite what many people may think about its evolution and whether companies will pay more attention to it and consequently invest more in it, the reality is that information security is a cost. And it is not just a simple cost, it is and can be a very heavy cost that could have devastating effects on the company brand and image if it is not properly secured.

In those conditions, unless some important changes happen, like new regulatory policies and procedures that will oblige companies to see security as an investment, we are afraid that security risks will only expand in their risk level and impact.

In addition, the authors of this book have tried to express their thoughts about the importance of placing people in the middle of the action and radically changing the current approach toward training and security awareness. The current approach simply does not work and change is mandatory; sooner or later developments will have to occur in order to better cope with risks.

We tend to forget that everything begins and ends with that special link, which is "humans." Oftentimes, we put the risk on software's or hardware's shoulders, forgetting that the human factor was the one that developed, programmed, and built all technological artifacts as we know them. So whatever might be insecure, in reality, humans have made so. The time to react and fix the basics is now. Some people argue that fixes should be done on the system level and that we should make those systems error free.

In this way, the human factor risk will be reduced and somehow overridden, which should lead to decreased security risks. Ideally, this outcome could come to be but the question is when have we (humans) ever made something 100% error/bug free? If an example can be found, then that is the way to go ahead. We are afraid that in the absence of this perfect, ideal information system, we will need to rely on people and change the way we provide information security awareness trainings. We need a radical approach where people will understand much more than the underlying threats and what impact they can cause; people need to be told about what's in it for them. Accountability and responsibility are the missing pieces in the story where the "I do not feel threatened. I do not really care" context is currently reigning.

Referencing Pareto's principle with regard to

information security and claiming that information security is 90% about people might be seen as a challenging statement. However, when we narrow down this idea to its core, and if we compare the most recent critical security breaches to it, we can easily conclude that human mistakes are what led to these devastating organizational outcomes. Moreover, with the recent explosion of connectivity; new technologies; and new ways to interact, socialize, and exchange information, all of the sudden, we have lost control of what is entering into and going out of the IT ecosystem. How can I control information that is outside of my organization's boundaries? Do I place a monitoring system on all social media websites to see what employees are communicating and with whom? Those are just some of the questions that need to be answered.

In the meantime, this book aims to open Pandora's box and change the current state of affairs. Something is very wrong with the way we currently manage security awareness trainings. It is clear that something in the process needs to be changed and this much-needed change will not be easy. It will ask for additional efforts and for an entire reset of outlooks from both the organizational and personal sides. If we want employees to care more, we will have to reinvent, redesign, and remodel current information security procedures and processes.

A great deal has been written, discussed, and argued about the right approach to solve this problem. While the debate will probably still continue for a long time, one thing is sure: acting now is a necessity and not acting may have devastating effects on today's and tomorrow's organizational foundations.

Information security should not be seen as a cost but rather as an investment. It is like when we develop a new product and we see it as a potential source of future revenue; security should be looked at in the same way— as a new product that is a cost-saving one and will help keep us from losing money.

Where will information security stand in few years' time? Looking at what is happening today, the current trends, and the security forecast, we can see a new era is coming where the topic of security will be omnipresent. Hopefully, this omnipresence will be a first step toward a new and different security culture where employees will be in the middle of the chain. Only by empowering employees and with the "inception" approach, where a security culture will be embedded right from the start, will we have good chances of decreasing security levels and increasing confidence in the information ecosystem.

Until we reach that nirvana, information security is and will remain 90% about humans and 10% about technology!

ABOUT THE AUTHORS

Mario Silic is an IT professional with over 20 years of experience in large international companies. His research motivation focuses on the fields of information security, open source software and mobile. He has published his work in several international journals and conferences.

dr.sc. Dario Silic is working in finance in an international corporation. He is professor in corporate finance and financial management at Zagreb School of Economics and Management.

www.ingramcontent.com/pod-product-compliance
Lightning Source LLC
Chambersburg PA
CBHW061026050326
40689CB00012B/2712